CW00615978

WONI

Mark Thomson

WONDROUS FLITTING

OBERON BOOKS
LONDON

WWW.OBERONBOOKS.COM

First published in 2011 by Oberon Books Ltd
521 Caledonian Road, London N7 9RH
Tel: +44 (0) 20 7607 3637 / Fax: +44 (0) 20 7607 3629
e-mail: info@oberonbooks.com
www.oberonbooks.com

A catalogue record for this book is available from the British
Library.

ISBN: 978-1-84943-211-5

Cover image © by Redpath Design

Printed in Great Britain by CPI Antony Rowe, Chippenham.

For Harry and Millie.

Characters

SAM
24, overweight.

DAD
Irish.

MUM

BOY
Eleven – twelve
years old.

GIRL (JULIE)
Eleven – twelve
years old.

GRANDDAD
At least eighty.

DENTIST

SHELLEY
Early – mid-
twenties.

CLEANER
(GLORIA)
Late twenties –
thirties.

VOICE
in a church.
Male.

JACKIE
Late thirties –
early forties.

JOHNNY
Late thirties –
early forties.

BUSINESS
WOMAN
Mid-forties.

GORDON
Voice only,
probably 50s.

Setting.
Something to suggest the intrusion of the wall.
Outskirts of a large contemporary city.

To be premiered by the Royal Lyceum Theatre Company at the Traverse during the Edinburgh Fringe Festival 2011 with the following team:

SAM Grant O'Rourke
ALL MALE PARTS Liam Brennan
ALL FEMALE PARTS Molly Innes

Director	Mark Thomson
Set & Lighting Design	Kai Fischer
Composer	Philip Pinksy
Costume Design	Lucy Minta Reeves
Assistant Director	Gareth Nicholls
DSM	Claire Williamson

1. THE HOUSE ARRIVES

Blasts and crashing. Music. Smoke. Clears to reveal SAM with a bowl of cereal. TV plays in the room. There is a section of bare brick wall that has cut through the living room wall of SAM's house. There is a pair of feet and legs in slippers sticking out from underneath the protruding wall.

SAM: Fuck me. Fuck me. Fuck me. Fucking hell. What's all that about then? Fucking wall. Fuck. That's a wall. Mum? *(Beat.)* Mum? Dad?

Moaning. Sees DAD's slippers sticking out from under the intruding wall.

SAM: Dad?

Moaning. SAM picks up his mobile. Can't get a signal.

SAM: Never. Just never. Dad. You ok? Dad? I can't get the – Can't get my – It's not. Dad? You ok? You ok, dad? Dad? Dad, you ok?

MUM: Son?

SAM: Mum?

MUM: Son?

SAM: That you mum?

MUM: Son?

SAM: Mum?

MUM: Son?

Beat.

SAM: You ok mum?

MUM: Son?

SAM: Mum?

MUM: S'that you son?

SAM: Mum?

MUM: Yes?

Beat.

SAM: Is dad in there mum?

MUM: Dad?

SAM: Mum?

MUM: Yes.

SAM: Is dad in there too mum?

MUM: Your dad?

SAM: Dad.

MUM: Dad.

SAM: Dad.

Beat.

MUM: I don't know.

SAM: You ok mum?

MUM: What?

SAM: You ok? Is dad in there?

MUM: Dad?

SAM: Yes.

MUM: I don't know. Are you ok?

SAM: Me?

MUM: Yes.

SAM: I'm fine. I'm just finishing my cereal.

MUM: Good boy.

SAM: I'm not a boy mum.

MUM: I know son.

SAM: Mum, what happened?

MUM: I don't know. It's completely dark.

SAM: Is it?

MUM: Can you see anything?

SAM: Yes.

MUM: What is it?

SAM: Well … you know where the living room wall is?

MUM: Yes, yes, I know that one.

SAM: Well there's another wall there.

MUM: The wall's changed?

SAM: No the old one's still there.

MUM: It's still there?

SAM: Oh yeah, it's still there but like there's another one there too.

MUM: Another wall?

SAM: Yeah.

MUM: Another wall?

SAM: It's kind of broken through our wall and into the living room. It's at an angle.

MUM: An angle?

SAM: Mum, I think I can see dad's feet.

MUM: His feet?

SAM: Like his feet, well they've got his slippers on so – well like they're under the wall.

MUM: Just his feet. Oh my God.

SAM: No it's not like they're detached. They're kind of jammed under the wall.

MUM: Oh my God.

SAM: The wall's weird mum. It's well … it's got weird writing and drawings and a cross with Jesus on it –

MUM: Jesus?

SAM: On a cross, you know one of those ones.

MUM: Like in a church?

SAM: Yeah – like that. I think.

MUM: Are they moving?

SAM: Moving?

MUM: Is your dad's feet moving.

SAM stares at them for a bit. They don't move.

SAM: No.

MUM: No?

SAM: No.

MUM: Oh my God.

SAM: Mum?

MUM: Son?

SAM: Mum, if I stand like right next to dad's feet and I keep talking and you move towards my voice you can maybe find dad, see if he's ok.

MUM: Ok son, but it is absolutely pitch dark in here, I can't see a thing. When are you going to start talking?

SAM: Will I do it now?

MUM: Ok start talking now. *(Beat.)* Son?

SAM: Sorry mum this is just a bit traumatic.

MUM: I know son keep calm.

SAM: I am but I just can't think of what to say.

MUM: That's it – keep talking.

SAM: Mum, what has happened? What is this wall doing in our house? I don't know how it got here. How could a wall come in our house?

MUM: Keep going son.

SAM: Where has this wall come from? And why –

DAD: Ow!

MUM: Dad?

SAM: Dad?

DAD: Oh, me arm.

MUM: I think I've stood on your dad.

SAM: Dad?

DAD: Stood on me arm.

SAM: Are you ok dad?

DAD: My legs. Can't move them.

SAM: Dad there's a wall in our house and it's on your legs.

DAD: A wall? How did that get here?

SAM: I don't know. It wasn't me.

DAD groans in pain as MUM stands on his arm again.

MUM: Sorry, I can't see anything.

DAD: Stay away from my arm.

MUM: I can't see where it is so how can I stay away from it.

DAD: Are you ok son?

SAM: I'm ok. I can't get a signal.

MUM: You can never get a signal here. Don't know why we don't change –

DAD: Oh don't get into that, the deal with Vodafone is absolutely the –

MUM: What's the point if we can't get a signal?

DAD: Sam just has to move to the back of the house.

MUM: How can he do that?

SAM: The wall's in the way dad, it's gone over the door to the hall too.

DAD: Well that's not Vodafone's fault is it?

SAM: Shut up!

Beat.

DAD: Now just stay calm son.

MUM: I don't like the dark. I don't like it when you shout at me, son.

SAM: Sorry mum.

DAD: I tell you what son, just relax – why don't you put the TV on?

SAM: Put the TV on?

DAD: Yes you like the TV.

SAM: I do like the TV.

DAD: Well there you are.

SAM: Ok.

DAD: Why don't we watch the news – we can just listen. That's something we like doing together. A bit of normality.

SAM: But dad, your legs.

DAD: Now don't you worry about my legs now, that's why we have doctors and, and whatever we do we can still do in five minutes' time. I don't like missing the news. You like the news don't you son?

SAM: It's all right.

DAD: That ok with you mum?

MUM: Yes.

SAM picks up the remote and looks the the TV on the wall. Instinctively switches it on. Sound of something like 'Friends' comes on but no picture. Distortion and interference. He stares at it.

SAM: There's a problem with the TV, dad. Oh God! Oh no!

DAD: Sounds fine to me, son.

SAM: No picture. The screen's not really ok, the wall … stuff.

DAD: Ok let's keep calm. Put in 925 and we can listen to radio 5.

SAM: What's radio 5?

DAD: It's like the news but no pictures.

SAM does as instructed. As it plays, SAM looks at shattered TV.

RADIO: – brings us to the extraordinary disappearance last night of the holy house of Loreto.

INTERVIEWER: which has stood on a hill on the Tuscan village of Loreto since 1294. The holy house is one of the world's most venerated Christian buildings, particularly for catholics who believe the house 'flitted' from Nazareth to its current home in Loretto. In the studio I have Ed Hollis, flitting house authority and author of 'The Secret Lives of Buildings.' Ed, the Catholic world is up in arms, the Pope is being urged to make a statement: the consternation at the house disappearing is astonishing. Can you give us a bit of background on this miraculous flitting house.

ED: You have to understand that this is the first time the holy house has 'moved' since 1294 when it arrived in Loretto.

INTERVIEWER: And it is strongly associated with miracles is it not? Read some for us, Ed.

ED: In 1631, there was a man called Joseph, covered in sores, unkempt, unshaven and unloved begging in the streets of Ancona in Italy. He had heard about a shrine nearby that was frequented by many pilgrims. Everyone knew the House was Holy; but they had no idea where it had come from, or what it was.

Not, of course that he was interested in pilgrimages: he had seen enough of the world to sneer at superstition. But he went.

Inside, the holy house contained one simple dark room. The walls had a greasy dampness to them; and they were bare, save for fragments of painting, and graffiti in a language that Joseph could not understand. At the east end of the House, in a flaming golden mandorla, resided a little baby, and his Mother, Our Lady.

He knelt with the other pilgrims at the altar and said his *Ave Marias*. When he emerged into the sunshine, he realised something was different. His lice and his sores and his filth had left him, and he had been made clean.

INTERVIEWER: So it moved from Nazareth to Loretto?

ED: No, no, nothing so straightforward. Myth has it, it first appeared to Shepherds in Croatia.

INTERVIEWER: It's fair to say then this house has flitted quite a few times.

ED: Oh yes.

I/VEWER: Tell us about its arrival in Loretto.

ED: In 1294, there was a virtuous matron called Laureta who lived in a grove of laurel trees. She had spent many years in solitude, praying to Our Lady amid the beasts of the forest and the wilderness.

One night, Laureta had a vision. Her grove was filled with light, and a small building descended from the heavens. As it touched down, the laurels of the grove bowed to the ground. The next morning she found that a clearing had appeared in her grove; and in the middle of that clearing there was now a small shrine with fragments of painting and graffiti on its walls.

INTERVIEWER: My favourite part of your book is when you describe its beginnings. It still makes the hairs stand up on the back of my neck to read it.

ED: Just over two thousand years ago, there was a small room about thirty-foot long and thirteen-foot wide in a little village.

The name of the village was Nazareth. In the house lived a girl named Mary. As Mary sat in her house, and to her great surprise, an angel flew in through the window on the western wall. His name was Gabriel. He said:

'Hail Mary, full of grace
The Lord is with thee.
Blessed art thou among women
And blessed is the fruit of thy womb, Jesus.'

And so
The Angel of the Lord appeared unto Mary
So, the house was the vessel that contained Mary, and Mary was the vessel that contained our Lord. So in the house,
The Word was made Flesh
And dwelt among us.
And like the practice of prayer, the Holy House comes for the faithful when they least expect it.

INTERVIEWER: Now to you unbelievers I understand that the house itself is made of stone and wood that only exists in Palestine. Is that right Ed?

ED: Indeed so.

INTERVIEWER: So where do you think it went last night with its graffitied and healing walls? Ed, why –

An electric crack comes from the smashed TV, a sure sign it is now fully dead.

DAD: It's a great reception you get on that radio on the TV, isn't it?

SAM walks to the wall, starts to feel it, looks at the mysterious writing, the cross.

DAD: So, we should think about getting some help.

SAM: Wait.

DAD: Good-o. No problem. No problem. Whenever you're ready is fine.

MUM: What's he going to do, do you think?

DAD: He'll get some help. Won't you son?

MUM: Get help!

DAD: We mustn't panic him.

MUM: I'm not going to panic him.

DAD: I didn't say you were. This is a delicate situation we're in here.

MUM: I don't like the dark.

DAD: I know.

SAM: Mum! Dad! This is … it's incredible. It's – wow. Dad, mum, it's – it's just.

DAD: What is it son?

SAM laughs joyously.

DAD: Are you ok son?

SAM: I don't know but we have been visited!

MUM: Oh thank God, who is it, your grandpa?

SAM: No mum, this is something else. You know what this means?

MUM: We need help?

SAM: This is way beyond that.

MUM: Beyond what?

SAM: This is much much bigger than help mum.

MUM: But we need help.

SAM: No mum, something has happened – don't you get it?

DAD: Try and stay calm –

SAM: Oh, this is it. I was waiting, you know, dad, waiting for something and I never ever knew if I was waiting or lost or maybe I was both and I knew something had to happen but I was like helpless or couldn't *see* it couldn't *find* what it *was* –

DAD: Now just slow down a wee bit till –

SAM: And now it's come, Oh God, it's come. Mum, dad, the holy house of Loretto is here!

MUM: What do you mean here?

SAM: It's *in* our house. Dad, it's on your legs. It's come to us. It's come to – I don't know, make us … I don't know – I don't know –

MUM: Just go and get help son, please.

SAM: Mum, the house where Christ was conceived by Mary has come to us. This is not about help.

MUM: What's it about?

SAM: I don't know. But I know it's come for a reason. God, I suddenly feel something.

DAD: What are you feeling son?

SAM: I can't describe it. I know if I go out there something is going to happen. Something is going to be, like transformed. Why has it come here?

DAD: How do you know it's the holy house son?

SAM: Didn't you hear, dad? It's gone – last night. No one knows where. And now – here. In our house.

DAD: My legs are going a bit numb.

SAM: Dad it's ok.

DAD: Son?

SAM: The holy house is upon them.

Beat.

DAD: That's true.

MUM: What do you mean?

SAM: Mum, it's come, we need to face it. What do I do? What do I do?

MUM: Go and get some help, son, Mrs Gilchrist will let you use her phone –

SAM: Mum, we can't rush into things.

MUM: No?

DAD: Listen to the boy.

SAM: When the holy house comes into your house you need to let it happen.

MUM: Let what happen?

SAM: Just let it happen. There's something else at work. We just need to let it work. It's a miracle. Mum, dad. We have been visited by a miracle.

DAD: My legs are definitely not feeling good.

SAM: Nothing can be wrong dad.

DAD: Ok, I know what you mean son, but –

SAM: It's *meaning*, dad. Dad, I'm twenty-four, I've no job I live with my parents – this is *it*.

MUM: What is it?

SAM: I think this is it. Got to go.

MUM: Where are you going?

DAD: Let the boy go.

MUM: But we're trapped in here.

DAD: You go son.

MUM: Oh my God.

DAD: He's got to do this.

MUM: Do what? Where are you going?

SAM: Mum, I'm just going.

DAD: Good luck son.

SAM: Thanks dad.

MUM: Oh my God.

2. KIDS

SAM is flitted to a road. Two children, maybe eleven or twelve on their mobile phones taking photographs of a flat and bloody dead animal. SAM stops and looks at the animal.

SAM: Is it dead?

GIRL: 'Is it dead?'

SAM: It's dead. Of course it's dead.

GIRL: What age are you?

SAM: I'm –

GIRL: Piss off, what would I want to know that for? He thinks I want to know what age he is.

BOY: What team do you support?

SAM: I don't. *(Alluding to boy's Chelsea top.)* So Rangers, eh?

BOY: No. Chelsea.

SAM: Chelsea?

BOY: So?

SAM: So not really local are they?

BOY: What's local got to do with it? I can support any team I want. Chelsea's in the Champion's League. Hey – can you smell something?

GIRL: Like what?

BOY: Like a loser.

GIRL: Oh man – that's stinkin'.

BOY: *(Looking at animal, lost in thought.)* I wish I'd seen it happen.

Pause.

BOY: Hey wee man, what is it do you think?

SAM: I don't know. Hard to tell with – with –

BOY: God you're useless.

GIRL: Useless cunt.

SAM: It's Tuesday. *(Beat.)* It's Tuesday. You must be about eleven. You should be at school.

Beat. They stare at him.

GIRL: Does he look like the social to you?

BOY: No, he doesn't.

GIRL: Look, what's your problem.

SAM: I'm just trying to see things, like allow them to affect me – see if I feel any different. Now. Today. I'm like open to it.

GIRL: Are you not well?

BOY: Talks like he's not well.

GIRL: You not well, boy?

SAM: How do you feel when you look at that animal?

GIRL: How do I feel?

SAM: I want to know.

GIRL: God, he sounds like my counsellor.

BOY: God.

GIRL: God.

SAM: Why you taking the photographs?

GIRL: I'm on blackberry messenger. He isn't.

BOY: So what?

SAM: That was alive! It was a living thing.

Beat.

BOY: You're well weird

GIRL: God.

BOY: God.

SAM: Because listen, I don't even know how I feel about that animal. I'm staring at it now and I'm trying to connect up – I'm opening myself up to the – the – whatever it is – was – and just, I don't know, allow myself to face what I actually feel. It's dead. I'm alive. It's gone. I'm not. I'm trying to unblock what's stopping me from *experiencing* what's passing between … us – me and it. Meaning. I'm telling you straight and not patronising you because you're kids. I've just had this *big thing* happen to me, you see, and I think it's about me not seeing things right, it's a cosmic wake up call for the formerly deaf; I want to tune in and not miss the call because I think it's come. *It's* come. I know I'm like rambling – but why has it come to *me*? What it means. What it means.

GIRL: You lookin' at my tits?

SAM: You don't have any tits.

GIRL: What?

SAM: *(Beat.)* You don't – you're about ten –

GIRL: Eleven.

SAM: You don't have any. That's what I see. That's it.

BOY: So you *were* lookin' at them.

GIRL: Just because I'm eleven doesn't mean I can't have tits. It's my right.

SAM: Look, you haven't –

GIRL: What a perv – he keeps going on about my tits, keeps talking about them.

SAM: How can I – you don't have any.

GIRL: See.

BOY: Fuckin' perv.

GIRL: Should I scream?

SAM: No!

GIRL: That's what the people who come into school say isn't it? Scream.

SAM: Don't!

GIRL: Stop looking at my tits!

SAM: I'm not!

GIRL: Should I scream?

BOY: Take a photo of him.

GIRL does so.

SAM: What'y'do that for?

GIRL: The world needs protected from paedos like you.

SAM: I'm not a paedo.

BOY: Paedo.

SAM: Look I'm sorry –

GIRL: Yeah, he's sorry now.

BOY: Too late now.

SAM: It's *not* too late.

BOY: Don't lose it with us just 'cause you're a paedo.

GIRL: Have you seen Jordan?

SAM: Jordan who?

GIRL: 'Jordan who.' You're weird.

SAM: You mean the glamour model.

GIRL: She's successful.

SAM: At what?

GIRL: She's *successful*. What you successful at?

SAM: Nothing.

GIRL: You seen her tits?

SAM: For God's sake.

GIRL: No?

SAM: *(Nervous.)* Of course I have.

GIRL: So you've seen them then? So you *know* Jordan.

SAM: I don't *know* her, I'm –

GIRL: You know her. *(To BOY.)* He's scared of us. Aren't you?

> *BOY takes a photo of SAM. They both sit down and start sending messages off.*

GIRL: Takes him ages to send stuff cause he's not got a blackberry.

BOY: Piss off.

GIRL: – off.

SAM: What you sending?

GIRL: Why don't you start showing some respect.

SAM: To you?

GIRL: Just 'cause I'm thirteen –

SAM: You said eleven.

GIRL: – Eleven doesn't mean I've not got rights. You stupid, boy?

BOY: We've got rights so don't start.

GIRL: Paedo.

BOY: Paedo.

SAM: That about me? You sending my photograph to people?

GIRL: Yes.

BOY: No, I'm just posting it on Facebook. Everybody should know about you.

GIRL: How many friends you got?

BOY: Eh, four hundred and eighty-three.

GIRL: That's ok.

BOY: I know it's ok.

GIRL: Fuck off then. Hey mister, you're a marked man.

SAM: You can't do that.

GIRL: S'done. Kids need protecting from people like you. Vulnerable people.

SAM: I haven't done anything. I think I've just seen a miracle.

GIRL: He's just called my tits a miracle.

BOY: Fuckin' paedo bastard..

SAM: Go away.

GIRL: Go away?

BOY: Go away?

GIRL: Right.

BOY: Right.

SAM: I just came to see the animal.

GIRL: *(Types into blackberry.)* 'Likes dead animals and little girls' tits.'

BOY: Let's go.

GIRL: I'm not sure.

BOY: C'mon.

GIRL: Not sure about leaving him here.

BOY: C'mon.

GIRL: Ok, chill man, chill. You're a marked man. What's your name?

SAM: Sam. *(Immediately regrets this.)*

GIRL: *(Types.)* 'Sam.'

BOY: *(Types.)* 'Sam the paedo.'

GIRL: Paedo.

The Children exit. SAM static. Looks down at the flattened animal. He takes out his phone and dials. It's an answerphone message.

SHELLEY: *(Voice.)* Hello, it's me Shelley: Sorry can't speak *(Muffled.)* A minute dad. Sorry can't speak right now but you can leave a message. Wait for the beep. Here it comes … Here – it – comes. *(Beeps over last word.)*

SAM: Hi. Hi Shelley, it's me. It's Sam. Can't remember are you working today? It's Tuesday. Tuesday, Tuesday – I think you sometimes – well, can you give me a bell? There's something happened and well – it's best if I talk to you in person. Can you give me a call back? Just going to my Granddad's and then I'm at the dentist's at 2.30 – the one on Derrick street, it's got pink windows or glass or something on the window to make it pink. Is it NHS? Why don't I think more about this stuff? See I'm changing, I'm thinking differently. I can feel a change, Shelley. I want to share it with you because it's trying to reveal something, like a cosmic invitation and I want to accept it and I, I love you and I want to –

He has been pacing and stood on the animal remains.

Oh, I've just – the animal – I've got to go. Call me? I'll … give me a call, but not before the dentist's 'cause you know I'm freaked out about … Anyway, bye. Bye.

He rings off and stares at the dead animal. He checks watch. Looks at the animal a long time. He finds a carrier bag in a bag he is carrying to put the animal in. He goes to pick it up. He finds something in his bag to scoop it up. It keeps sliding off. An eyeball pops out and rolls away. He manages to scoop animal up and after failing to scoop up eyeball picks it up with his fingers. He goes back to wall. Looks at it.

3. GRANDDAD

SAM is flitted to his GRANDDAD's house. He is either immaculate in a suit and shirt with v-necked pullover or in a vest with tattoos on his arm. He is in an electric wheelchair. SAM is bathing his eyes with a sponge.

SAM: Can you open them yet, Granddad?

GRANDDAD: No.

SAM: Are you trying?

GRANDDAD: Yes.

SAM: I've put loads on.

GRANDDAD: Put more on.

SAM: It's like going on your jumper.

GRANDDAD: More. Little bitch.

SAM: What?

GRANDDAD: Didn't come at all yesterday, she didn't. Supposed to come in twice a day. Knows I'm here on my own. NHS eh? NHS.

SAM: I know.

GRANDDAD: No you don't. Woke up this morning and couldn't open them a bit. Jammed shut. You get the cataracts cut out and then your eyelids stick to your eyeballs. What's the point of that? Who voted that lot in, eh? Did you?

SAM: What?

GRANDDAD: Did you vote them in?

SAM: I … I don't know. Can't remember. Probably not.

GRANDDAD: So I'm stuck here.

SAM: I like here. I like you being here like you've always been.

GRANDDAD: I know, son. I like you being here too. You're a good boy.

SAM: I like the way it looks, I like the rooms. I like the smell.

GRANDDAD: What smell?

SAM: The smell of your house.

GRANDDAD: It's got a smell?

SAM: Yeah.

GRANDDAD: What's it smell like?

SAM: Hard to describe a smell.

GRANDDAD: Smells like what?

SAM: Don't know – you I suppose.

GRANDDAD takes this in. He suddenly loses it and shoots off in his wheelchair banging into something.

GRANDDAD: Bloody stinking arsehole NHS bastards blind blind blind blind blind!

SAM: You ok?

GRANDDAD: No I'm not ok. I can't see. I don't want this, I don't want to live here any more, I don't know what this world's up to and now it's gone and forgotten me and time was, and I don't mean to bad mouth your mother, but time was your kin – they'd take care of you in your old age, that's how it works, since the time of the cavemen and cave women. Oh, don't listen to me, son, I've had enough. Did you pass them on your way here?

SAM: Pass who?

GRANDDAD: Just them. *(Beat.)* Whole street's changed. Like it's a different shape. Like it's turned into another place. Even the smell of it. But I'm still here. But it's not.

SAM: I –

GRANDDAD: Everyone stayed near then. Could see my tribe, could feel my tribe all about me, feel it at the back of everything you did, why you did it, when to do it. You could *see* each other. Maybe a few streets away but there was a vein that rode through the streets in and out of houses where your family lived. You shouted loudly enough out your front door and they'd know about it they would. Next thing blood would come through the door. And everything would be sorted again. Whatever the problem.

SAM: What kind of problems, Granddad?

GRANDDAD: Doesn't matter.

SAM: Like what?

GRANDDAD: Look son, anything. *Anything*. See? That's the point.

SAM: I see.

GRANDDAD: Right.

SAM: I see.

GRANDDAD: Now there's all these people I don't know. They come from bloody everywhere. Take our houses. I can't even understand them. All those languages. All those colours. They don't know who I am. They don't know me.

SAM: You should just introduce yourself, Granddad, they're –

GRANDDAD: But I don't want to. I don't know what this place is now. Where's my tribe? What is this place? What's it for? What's it supposed to be? I didn't fight Hitler for that! *(Beat.)* And where is everyone now? Where is the family? All over the place. Everyone is not where they started. They're off somewhere else. Your sister's gone off. Where is she?

SAM: Birmingham.

GRANDDAD: Birmingham. Good God, Birmingham, eh? Birmingham?

SAM: Yeah – she's in Birmingham now. She was in Coventry.

GRANDDAD: Coventry?

SAM: Yeah – she was in Coventry before.

GRANDDAD: Good God.

SAM: Yeah. *(Beat.)* Before that she was –

GRANDDAD: But not you.

SAM: What?

GRANDDAD: You. Not gone anywhere.

SAM: No. I'm still here.

GRANDDAD: Still here, eh?

SAM: Yeah.

GRANDDAD: Still here.

SAM: Yeah.

GRANDDAD: Well get out there and see the world! *(Beat.)* My bag needs changing.

SAM: I don't know how to do that, Granddad.

GRANDDAD: No?

SAM: No.

GRANDDAD: Should change it really. Bad not to.

SAM: I don't know if I can.

GRANDDAD: You walk outside now and shout for help there's no blood running into your home. Just looks like, surprised, or put on. Who's the old man? Who's the old white man.

SAM: Now granddad –

GRANDDAD: In Indian or African or Polish, loads of Polish or Russians or Romanians, who's the old man and even them born here, like British, they're not from here and they don't know you either –

SAM: Granddad the world has –

GRANDDAD: Do you know how frightening that is? I don't care about your, 'now Granddad' Rubbish. I know how I feel. I know. S'why I did the pamphlets for the last twenty year.

SAM: I don't think the BNP are the answer, Granddad.

GRANDDAD: You don't have the answer. What answer you got for me? Words words words. They don't mean anything, son. The people saying them don't know what it means. They don't believe it. They just think they should.

SAM: Granddad, something happened this morning.

GRANDDAD: What?

SAM: A miracle.

GRANDDAD: You got a job? Sorry, son, forget that – still a bit worked up with my eyes and bag and all. What happened, tell your old granddad. He's here for you.

SAM: There's a holy house from Italy and it has landed inside our house.

GRANDDAD: Is it Catholic then?

SAM: I suppose – yes.

GRANDDAD: Right.

SAM: This has happened to me. To me.

GRANDDAD: Are you on drugs, son?

SAM: No!

GRANDDAD: So this Catholic church is in your house?

SAM: Yes.

GRANDDAD: What's your mother and father got to say about that?

SAM: Well they're jammed in their bedroom. In fact there's a bit of it *on* my dad.

GRANDDAD: Is he alive?

SAM: Says he's fine. I wanted to come here first, granddad and let you know. I need to know why this has happened to me.

GRANDDAD: Well you would.

SAM: Yeah.

GRANDDAD: You sure it's this holy house –

SAM: Certain. It was on the news – it's disappeared. Seems like this house disappeared before like from Israel or something and ended up in Italy. Until now.

GRANDDAD: I fucking hate this.

SAM: What?

GRANDDAD: I hate what it's becoming.

SAM: Like what.

GRANDDAD: I don't see why things have got like this. I don't see how things are better.

SAM: Can I get you anything, Granddad?

GRANDDAD: I need my bag changed.

SAM: I can't do that.

GRANDDAD: Why not?

SAM: I can't do that.

GRANDDAD: What age are you?

SAM: Twenty-four.

GRANDDAD: Then you don't want to do it.

SAM: No, I don't know how.

GRANDDAD: I can talk you through it.

SAM: S'fine.

GRANDDAD: Then you don't want to – what do you want to do, son?

SAM: In what way?

GRANDDAD: Well now you're twenty-four and you are
probably through the, 'I want to be a fireman or footballer
or prime minister' phase, what do you want. *(Beat.)*

SAM: If I took you to the house maybe it could heal you. It
could make you see. I know I sound mad granddad but I
think it's been sent to me.

GRANDDAD: There's nothing wrong with me.

SAM: I know but –

GRANDDAD: I'm not the problem. *(Beat.)*

SAM: Ok.

GRANDDAD: Ok.

SAM: Ok.

GRANDDAD: You can go now.

SAM: Ok. Is there anything –

GRANDDAD: Only my bag.

SAM: Right. Well. Well I'll see you soon, Granddad. *(Beat.)* I
hope your eyes, you know …

GRANDAD exits, bumping into things as he goes.

4. THE DENTIST'S SURGERY

*SAM flits to the dentist's surgery. He realizes he has a bag with a dead
animal in it. He looks for somewhere to hide it. Fails. He tries to make
the bag sit nicely. Fails. A DENTIST wheels in a dental chair and a
trolley of instruments.*

DENTIST: Who are you? I don't know you. Are you one of
mine? Right, right, right. Ok. I've no receptionist. Off.
She's off. She's off with stress. I don't know why? Why? I
don't know – why is her son off school? He's always off. Is
that stress too? Is her son off with stress? What's the time?

God. I'm – I'm behind. How did that happen? Have you filled in a form?

SAM: Sorry, no.

DENTIST: No?

SAM: No.

DENTIST: No form?

SAM: No.

DENTIST: So how …?

SAM: Sorry?

DENTIST: How are we going to do this?

SAM: What do you mean?

DENTIST: Well how can I see you?

SAM: I'm here.

DENTIST: Well, are you?

SAM: What?

DENTIST: What's the time?

SAM: It's nearly quarter to three..

DENTIST: It's what?

SAM: Nearly quarter to –

DENTIST: Already?

SAM: Yes.

DENTIST: Well why didn't you? Oh God.

SAM: Look why don't I go and come back another day. This is the first time in eight years I've come to the dentists, I'm really nervous and if you're rushed –

DENTIST: But you're in the book.

SAM: I suppose I –

DENTIST: You're in the book.

SAM: I know I made an –

DENTIST: But you've not got a form.

SAM: No.

DENTIST: You're in the book but you've not got a form. *(Beat.)* Sit down! Come on, sit down. My receptionist is off with stress.

SAM: Yes, you told me that.

DENTIST: What do you think of that?

SAM: I don't know her.

DENTIST: Don't you?

SAM: This is my first time here.

DENTIST: God, god, it's almost three. Open your mouth please. Just relax. Just relax. A-ha.

SAM: God.

DENTIST: Almost three!

SAM: You are NHS aren't you?

DENTIST: Yes.

SAM: Only I just wouldn't feel comfortable otherwise. Not if you weren't treating NHS patients.

DENTIST: So that's my value to you? My value to you is that I don't charge you properly?

SAM: I don't mean it like that, doctor.

DENTIST: I'm a dentist! You want my value as low as it can be, is that it?

SAM: I'm trying to figure out a bigger picture, you know what I mean?

DENTIST: And a smaller fee. For me, for me, yes?

SAM: I just think if you're not treating, you know, the poor people then I couldn't sit here. I've just realized that, just now, right now.

DENTIST: Well don't.

SAM: What do you mean?

DENTIST: Get up and walk out. Walk tall.

SAM: Look, I know this has nothing to do with you and you'll probably think I'm a bit, ha, well, a bit – but nothing is the same now, it'll never be again, and I think all I need to do is like, be aware and be open to *seeing* things differently, *listen* to what it's telling me.

DENTIST: You should have filled in a form!

SAM: I know, but –

DENTIST: A fucking form – what's your name –

SAM: Sam.

DENTIST: A fucking form, Sam, you could start with just playing the game a little bit. Where's your sense of community? I'm behind, Sam, I'm behind and you want to talk metaphysics. My assistant is off with stress.

SAM: I'm sorry, how is she?

DENTIST: She's *stressed*. She's stressed Sam because that's what happens.

SAM: But why does it happen? Why is this happening?

DENTIST: Why is what happening?

SAM: What?

Beat.

DENTIST: I don't know how to do the forms.

SAM: That's ok.

DENTIST: It's not. It's not ok. I don't know why, but it's not ok.

SAM: It's ok.

DENTIST: Is it?

SAM: How can it not be.

DENTIST: How can what not be?

SAM: What?

Beat.

SAM: There's a church that moved from Nazareth to Loreto hundreds of years ago, like carried by angels, for God, and I think it just landed in my house this morning.

DENTIST: All right.

SAM: It's a miracle. I've got nothing. There's nothing I – apart from Shelley, my girlfriend, we've talked about getting married – but I spend hours in my room playing games and looking at the TV and I sleep loads, and why do I sleep loads, because … I don't know why I sleep loads. I sometimes just decide to sleep in the middle of the day. Because I can. I go on Facebook. I surf a bit. I sometimes go out. I go out with Shelley. I look out my window. And I try and figure out what the reason just to go outside would be and I can't grasp it. But then sometimes I do go out. I try for jobs. The jobs are … not good. But I should. But why? Why? Why?

DENTIST: *(Far away.)* Teeth.

SAM: Teeth?

DENTIST: You're here for teeth.

SAM: Right, yes, right.

DENTIST: I am now so far behind. I am so far. I am so far behind.

SAM: I'm sorry.

DENTIST: That's all right.

SAM: Sorry.

DENTIST: It doesn't matter. Everything is fine.

SAM: It's just been in my head.

DENTIST: And now it's in mine too.

SAM: It's just good to talk, you know.

DENTIST: Yes.

SAM: How can we find out what we think or what we are if we don't talk.

DENTIST: *(Far away.)* Teeth. Oh yes. Teeth.

SAM: Sorry, yes, my teeth.

DENTIST: Don't worry, everything will be all right.

SAM: Er, yes, well I do hope –

DENTIST: It's all right.

SAM: Good.

DENTIST: It's all right.

SAM: Right.

DENTIST: *(Snappily coming to.)* Open up. Let's have a look. Jesus Christ.

SAM: I know.

DENTIST: What a disaster zone.

SAM: Please don't say that, I said I'm really nervous about –

DENTIST: Jesus Mary and –

SAM: Ok, ok.

DENTIST: Wide.

SAM: *(Mouth open.)* Ah-ha.

DENTIST: Am I your dentist?

SAM: Yes, you're my dentist.

DENTIST: But you come in here and you don't treat me like a dentist. Instead – wide – you treat me like I am some kind of rubbish tip for your existentialist manure.

SAM: I don't need this.

DENTIST: People don't know what they need.

SAM: Oh come on –

DENTIST: Stop! I can't move into these 'Oh Come on now what's that about oh you never did bullshit banality.' I'm on a different level now, I'm moving on and I'm beginning to see just how we waste breath, precious human breath, evasion, petty desires, petty petty petty small change fearful and escape – lost meaningfully – what a misuse of that force, 'will' when all the world and you in the world with its and your colours bend and shift toward revelation and light. You know I could really hurt you with this fucker.

SAM: Look you're really freaking me out. I've had a lot to deal with already today and I don't think it's right that dentists should talk like this.

DENTIST: So how should dentists talk?

SAM: Well, 'Open your mouth. This is going to hurt just a little bit' – and not 'you fucker.'

DENTIST: You know, this *is* going to hurt a bit –

SAM: *(Up off chair.)* Now I told you that I was very nervous when I came in here and in fact, in fact I told you it had been eight years since I'd been at *any* dentist's. And I said, please, I have an inordinate fear of dentists, even looking at the chair and the minty chemical smell makes me dizzy.

DENTIST: Then get off the chair – fuck your teeth!

SAM: 'Fuck my – ' Do you know how much courage it took to walk through that door, your door and put myself into your hands.

DENTIST: Fuck them.

SAM: You're a dentist. You – you can't say that.

DENTIST: I've broken through.

SAM: I could report you.

DENTIST: You didn't fill in a form. It doesn't matter.

SAM: Yes it does.

DENTIST: Wide! Ha – now there's your fear.

SAM: What?

DENTIST: Let me make you a set of teeth to go with your own.

SAM: Do I need it?

DENTIST: Need has gone! I know you. Do you know you? Yes-yes-yes you need it – God you need it.

SAM: What will happen if I don't – I mean what are my options – what can I expect to happen if I don't get them?

DENTIST: Nothing.

SAM: Then how – so look – what would I want to do that for – for nothing?

DENTIST: Because nothing will happen. Look I'm not God: you can't expect me to have all the answers. Have you no part to play in this, no responsibility.

SAM: I'm trying to *take* responsibility! I don't *want* dental work if I don't need it.

DENTIST: You do need it.

SHELLEY: *(Burst in.)* Sam, I wonder if we should split up.

SAM: Shelley? What are you –

SHELLEY: I know we've not been too happy. Sam, I've got Chlamydia. I've got a veneral disease, Sam. For God's sake how do you expect us to just carry on? What are you thinking?

SAM: You've got chlamydia?

SHELLEY: Now do you get it. You ready to face that, Sam? Ready to face your responsibilities now?

DENTIST: Wide.

SAM: But I haven't done anything, Shell, honestly I haven't. There's no way –

SHELLEY: No I know, it was me that did it. For God's sake.

SAM: How – why?

SHELLEY: Oh, what does it matter.

SAM: What does it matter? Shell, we've been together for two years, we're engaged.

DENTIST: Oh so so banal.

SAM: Look I don't think this is the best time to be talking about this.

DENTIST: Teeth.

SHELLEY: I've been speaking to my mother –

SAM: Oh well, right, so, that's all clear then.

SHELLEY: I don't think that's fair. Sam, my mother had chlamydia too.

DENTIST: Mother and daughter in diseased love triangle.

SAM: I don't care if your mum had chlamydia.

SHELLEY: Well maybe that's the problem, Sam, because what do you really care about at all, because it matters, it really matters.

SAM: I'm not saying it doesn't.

DENTIST: You need to take hold of this.

SAM: How?

SHELLEY: Have you noticed we don't really look at each other when we talk?

SAM: No, no, I don't think that's – well, if it is then –

SHELLEY: Sam, calm down.

SAM: *(Not not calm at all.)* What?

DENTIST: Don't calm down – risk the consequences of your temper. Stop editing! Let yourself pass through yourself.

SAM: But I'm not even – Shelley, I love you.

SHELLEY: Woops.

SAM: What do you mean Woops?

SHELLEY: It's like when someone's dropped something that isn't true or right.

SAM: That's what 'woops' is?

SHELLEY: Yes, I made it up and I think it's going to help me.

DENTIST: Is it too obvious for me to suggest immediate extraction?

SAM: Shelley we have a lot in –

SHELLEY: Woops.

SAM: Well we do, think of all the –

SHELLEY: Woops.

SAM: We've got something –

SHELLEY: Woops.

SAM: That's not helping.

SHELLEY: Now, Sam, I'm going to go now. My mum's waiting for me. *(To DENTIST.)* There was no one out there when we came in. There are three people waiting.

DENTIST: My receptionist is off with stress.

SHELLEY: But I can't help that.

DENTIST: Then who can?

SHELLEY: I can't solve this problem for you. *(To SAM.)* Sam, mum's waiting and there are no magazines so she'll be getting agitated.

SAM: What a surprise.

SHELLEY: Woops. And so you can get on with your day and not worry about me or –

SAM: Can't we just talk –

SHELLEY: No Sam. I don't want to do that so no, I won't and that feels really nice, you know, and I see that right now you can't be happy for me, but maybe some day. But I feel nice Sam, really, really nice.

SAM: Oh God.

SHELLEY: It's nice, Sam, it really is.

SAM: So nothing I can say –

SHELLEY: That's right, but in many ways that's what helps all this because I am so clear, Sam, and that's good for me and I know you can't see or feel that right now but it's good for you too.

SAM: Shelley, can I call you later?

SHELLEY: No, Sam.

SAM: But I am your Byron.

DENTIST: God.

SHELLEY: No, Sam.

SAM: Please let –

SHELLEY: Woops.

SAM: We can work it –

SHELLEY: Woops.

SAM: Shelley …

SHELLEY: Woops.

SHELLEY exits. The DENTIST has a drill or instrument in his hand. DENTIST cries. No one moves. SAM picks up his bag. It is dripping with blood. DENTIST pulls out one of his own front teeth.

DENTIST: It's all right. It's all right.

DENTISTS takes off tray and dental chair.

5. CLEANER

SAM flits to a church. There is a CLEANER there. She is Polish.

SAM: Hello? Hello? Hello?

CLEANER: This has to stop.

SAM: What's that?

CLEANER: Stop stop stop.

SAM: I saw outside, there was a poster saying Jesus died so you could get a life. I came in so I could speak to a priest or someone.

CLEANER: Stop enough enough. *(In Polish.)*

SAM: I need advice on –

CLEANER: No one is here. He's never here. I don't know where he is.

SAM: – on a miracle that I think has happened. He's not here?

CLEANER: A miracle?

SAM: Well, yes.

CLEANER: Are you one of the mad ones?

SAM: I don't think so.

CLEANER: You don't sound very sure. The man here, he is not here. Troubles.

CLEANER gets up and starts to wash the floor or something.

CLEANER: *(In Polish, agitated.)* This has to stop. This has to stop. Enough of this. This has to stop.

SAM: Do you need help?

CLEANER: No you can't help.

SAM: Maybe I can. Can I try?

CLEANER: Did I ask you?

SAM: No, but I'm offering.

CLEANER: How good you must feel.

SAM: I don't feel good.

CLEANER: Oh you don't feel good.

SAM: No. Can I try – to help?

CLEANER: You're like a movie. Like a film talking. Did you hear that on a film and think I must say that sometime, to someone and see what it feels like. Except that I'd need to be stupid and about five or six to chat to 'Can I try' man. Is that who you are?

SAM: But at least I am trying? Is that wrong?

CLEANER: Good boy.

SAM: I'm not a boy. Stop calling me that! Let's start again.

CLEANER: No, let's not start again, let's not bother. I'm a cleaner.

SAM: That's fine.

CLEANER: Is it? Thanks. My hands are bad. I clean lots of places. Hands bad, yeah. Hard hard hands. Look at the colour of them. Look at my face. Look at my leg. That colour's not mine.

SAM: We need a cleaner.

CLEANER: Do you?

SAM: There's a house in our house. It's made a terrible mess.

CLEANER: How did the house get in your house?

SAM: You know, I like things to be clean.

CLEANER: You'd like me then.

SAM: I don't know.

CLEANER: I make something you like.

SAM: I just like things being clean that's all. I don't like cleaning though.

CLEANER: Ah.

SAM: I know how that sounds.

CLEANER: You like things to be clean.

SAM: Yes. Yes, I do.

CLEANER: I'm your dream girl.

SAM: No, you're not.

CLEANER: Ok, I'm not.

SAM: Well you could be.

CLEANER: Well make up your mind I've not got all day.

SAM: I thought I knew who I wanted. But …

CLEANER: But she didn't want you? Another film.

SAM: But she's got chlamydia.

CLEANER: Oh, right.

SAM: And now it's over.

CLEANER: You give her chlamydia. Next time you give the woman chocolates or flowers.

SAM: No, I didn't give it to her she got it somewhere else, like from someone else. And now it's gone.

CLEANER: The chlamydia?

SAM: No – 'us.' We're gone. Things today – just appearing. And then they disappear.

CLEANER: She's a cunt.

SAM: What?

CLEANER: She's a cunt. Chlamydia girl.

SAM: I don't like that word.

CLEANER: That doesn't mean she isn't one.

SAM: Doesn't mean she is.

CLEANER: What?

SAM: A – I'm not saying that.

CLEANER: Why – is it a dirty word?

SAM: Yes.

CLEANER: It make you feel dirty, the word?

SAM: Of course.

CLEANER: No, not of course. Don't say of course. Lazy boy.

SAM: Everybody knows that word is vile.

CLEANER: Do they?

SAM: Yes.

CLEANER: You want to stay on the inside, yes? Yes you do, lazy boy.

SAM: How do you know I'm lazy.

CLEANER: Stay on the inside, lazy boy.

SAM: I don't like you calling me that.

CLEANER: So lots of 'I don't likes' I hear from you. What you like?

Beat.

SAM: There's lots of things I like.

CLEANER: Like?

SAM: You're just a cleaner, why are you lecturing me about what's right and wrong and telling me what I think or don't.

CLEANER: What age are you, lazy boy?

SAM: Twenty-four.

CLEANER: That's a nice age. But too old to know nothing and to have done nothing.

SAM: How do you know I've done nothing.

CLEANER: The way you walk. Rabbit eyes. The way your head drops for no reason except that there is nothing keeping it up. The way you speak tells me every morning you wake up and your petty, endless foreplay with the day has you biting at the wind as your belly gets fat with emptiness, your words all fat with emptiness.

SAM: Did you call me fat?

CLEANER: Of course I called you fat.

SAM: You are very cruel.

CLEANER: There is no cruelty in a truth that is delivered with a kiss.

She kisses him.

CLEANER: I mean you well, my fat lazy boy.

SAM: Maybe it's me that needs cleaned.

CLEANER: Or your girlfriend. Some antibiotics.

SAM: Maybe I need cleaned.

CLEANER: We all need cleaned.

SAM: Like from the inside, just wiped clean, all the bad stuff bounced out of my head, not messed up with noise and pictures and feelings. Just clean.

CLEANER: We all need cleaned.

SAM: Yes, I know you're right. But I don't know what you mean.

CLEANER: Aren't those the best truths? Do you want me to clean you?

SAM: *(Beat.)* Yes.

CLEANER: How?

SAM: I just want to be clean. What's your name?

CLEANER: Gloria. And yours?

CLEANER: It's Sam.

CLEANER: Ok Sam.

> *She takes his t-shirt off, takes out a clean cloth and washes his face and torso. CLEANER sits and hands him the cloth. SAM takes it and slowly takes her shoes off and washes her feet and legs. Perhaps she sings a song. Eventually she gets up and leaves.*
>
> *The shadow of a figure in a robe.*

6. HOME FOR THE SECOND TIME

SAM flits to his home. Stands there. He is carrying chip suppers or McDonalds.

DAD: Son?

MUM: Son?

DAD: Son, is that you? Son?

SAM: It's just me dad. You still here?

MUM: Still here.

DAD: Still hanging in there.

SAM: Oh, good.

DAD: How was your day, son? How did your day go for you?

SAM: It didn't go like I thought it might or like I maybe wanted it to.

DAD: Well, I'm sorry to hear that.

MUM: Ours wasn't too good either.

DAD: Now, mum, there's no point, what's the point in all that?

MUM: And what about your legs?

DAD: No pain.

MUM: Is that no pain or no feeling at all.

DAD: It amounts to the same thing.

MUM: It does not.

SAM: I've come home.

DAD: Well that's good then.

MUM: Have you brought anybody?

DAD: No mum.

MUM: Sam, have you brought anybody?

SAM: Why?

MUM: Well, about the house son, the wall, your dad's legs.

DAD: Stop, will you he's just got in the door –

MUM: But he's –

DAD: Now let the boy in, will you, before settling all your demands on his shoulders.

MUM: God.

DAD: Did you find what you were looking for?

SAM: I don't know.

DAD: Well, that's fine, that's the way it is sometimes with days. You just 'don't know.' Is that how it is?

SAM: Yes.

MUM: I can tell you how our day was if you like.

DAD: Will you stop that!

SAM: I came back. I brought you some food.

SAM walks towards the wall and discovers the impossibility of the task.

MUM: What's he doing?

DAD: Well I can't see him now, can I mum?

Growling.

MUM: Oh God, there it is again. I tell you I can hear something in here.

DAD: How could there be anything it's our bedroom.

MUM: I can hear something.

DAD: It'll be outside

MUM: It's inside.

DAD: It's outside.

SAM: *(Checking the remote.)* The TV's not working dad.

DAD: I know, son, terrible, terrible.

MUM: What's happening to your dad's legs – that's terrible.

DAD: Stop putting pressure on –

SAM: It heals people dad. The holy house. Ed said.

DAD: Yes, it seems so.

SAM: It heals.

MUM: Well something's going to have to heal your legs because I can't hear any ambulance.

DAD: Did you hear the boy, the house is a healing house.

SAM: But it goes. It goes if we don't take care. Dad, it heals. It can heal.

DAD: Yes, that seems to be the case.

SAM: Because I think I might need healing, dad.

DAD: Well, there you are, then.

SAM: I might need that.

   Pause.

SAM: Dad?

DAD: Yes son?

SAM: Dad.

DAD: Yes son, I'm here for you.

SAM: I know because I didn't get help to get you out of there.

DAD: That's ok son.

SAM: Is it?

DAD: Don't you worry your head about it.

SAM: Dad.

DAD: Yes son.

SAM: Dad – I'm fat.

Beat.

MUM: Now –

DAD: Well wait a minute he's talking to me now.

MUM: Yes but –

DAD: Let me have a –

MUM: But I'm his mum.

DAD: The boy's just said to me he feels fat.

A snigger off. Oddly amplified.

MUM: I know that – God – I heard him as well. I am here too.

DAD: Do you have to involve yourself in everything I do –

MUM: Oh, for goodness sake this isn't about *you*.

DAD: No, it's about our son.

MUM: That's right – our son.

DAD: That's right.

MUM: Right, who has just opened up and said he's fat.

Snigger off. Growling.

DAD: He's not – don't say that.

MUM: I didn't say that – he did.

DAD: But you're talking like you think he is.

MUM: I did not.

MUM: Son, you don't think that do you? You know what I meant.

Silence.

DAD: You've made him go all quiet again.

MUM: *I* did?

SAM: *(Loud.)* I'm fat.

Snigger. Silence.

SAM: I'm fat.

DAD: See – he's still saying he's fat.

MUM: He says he's fat. He *said* he's fat.

DAD: Yes.

MUM: Well then.

DAD: What?

MUM: You're not fat, son.

SAM: I'm fat. I'm fat. I'm fat. I'm fat. I'm fat. I'm fat. I'm fat. I'm fat. I'm fat. I'm fat. I'm fat. I am fat. Fat I am. I'm, I'm, I'm fat. I'm fat. I'm fat.

Snigger. Growling.

DAD: That wasn't your mum who laughed.

MUM: I think he knows I wouldn't laugh about something so serious.

DAD: It's not serious, goodness sake, what are you saying?

MUM: I mean to him.

DAD: But your saying it's serious is just going to build it right up in his head. That's cancer that is.

SAM: I'm fat.

VOICE: *(Harsh, sharp.)* Fat Sam fucking deal with it can feel you sitting, a lump of fat paralysis fuck.

Beat.

MUM: Fat paralysis? What is that? I told you I could hear something. Son, I don't want to be in here with him – did you hear the things he was saying. Let me out. Let me out son and we can sort everything out and forget –

DAD: Maybe he doesn't want to forget about the whole thing. He's on a sort of mission, aren't you son and he's just said things for mum and dad –

SAM: I'm fat.

DAD: Like he's fat – says he's fat.

VOICE: He *IS* fat.

MUM: Now, he says he's fat.

SAM: God. God on a hilltop bound up in molecules of mist hidden and breathed in –

MUM: That is beautiful, son, it's –

SAM: – What an offer that would be – like I could rise out of all this knowing that wherever I've wandered and got lost I know that it led to something. Even when you're lost you know it leads to something wonderful. 'Cause you know that and you can move around, find your way. Find your way back. Find your way forward. Healing –

Growl.

VOICE: Go on a diet.

SAM: Who's that?

MUM: We don't know.

DAD: Well, you see the light sort of smashed when the holy house landed on top of us, well inside our house. Whatever. Now don't you worry we're perfectly able to be in the dark –

MUM: So we can't see anything.

Snigger. MUM and DAD whispering.

DAD: Son, I think it's fair to say son that your mum and I think it may be a malevolent presence.

SAM: But it's a holy house. How?

MUM: No idea. Absolutely no idea. Just slipped in, in the dark.

DAD: I think it may be time to call the authorities and get us out of here son.

SAM: But I think we know now, dad, there is a higher authority. Otherwise we're just animals eating each other and surviving.

MUM: Nothing wrong with that. Nothing wrong with surviving!

DAD: Absolutely get that, son, but I do think, you know with my legs, and that's no fault of yours at all – an accident entirely, well we may be getting near to the touch and go point.

SAM: But the wrong authority might make it flit again. It's happened before it said on the TV. We need to know why it's come. I need healed –

DAD: And we are entirely supportive in you finding what it is and the healing –

MUM: Let us out. Let us out!

SAM: I'm fat.

MUM: Let us out!

SAM: I'm fat.

DAD: You are you son.

SAM: I just want to be me.

DAD: That's right, son.

SAM: I just want to be me! Just let me be me. Let me find what ME MEANS!

DAD: No problem. No problem at all. We will support you in whatever you do.

MUM: Let us out!

SAM: Why?

DAD: Why?

MUM: Because I want out.

SAM: What if I kill someone, what if I kill granddad and bring him here and eat him.

DAD: *(Beat.)* Hypothetically –

MUM: That's a terrible thing to say. Don't say these things.

SAM: What if I set fire to the house, now, would you support me in that?

Snigger. Beat.

DAD: Probably not.

SAM: Why?

DAD: Conflict of interests.

SAM: *Your* interests.

MUM: Yes – *ours.*

SAM: So where's the line?

DAD: Which line is that, son?

SAM: The line I can't cross. When your support disappears. When it stops being ok. Where is the line, dad, where?!

VOICE: Get out! Ohhhhh you – what – Christ. Christ. Out! Out! Get out of here!

MUM: Oh God.

VOICE: Get fucking oh fat fuck get the fuck fucking out I am God. Alight. Alight! I am God!

SAM: I'm going.

MUM: Oh God.

SAM: I'm going!

MUM: Please! Let us out! Let us out! Let us out! Please. Let us out! Let us out!

SAM has gone. Growling. Snigger.

MUM: Can you see anything? Dad? *(Beat.) Dad?*

Growling.

7. EVENING SCENE AT SHELLEY'S HOUSE

A man, SHELLEY's FATHER, is sitting in a chair staring at the TV. It is MTV.

SAM: Mr Donnelly. Mr Donnelly. The door was … I'm here to see Shelley.

FATHER: So?

SAM: I need to speak to her.

FATHER: Ok then.

SAM: Can I see her?

FATHER: Do what you want.

SAM: Where is she?

FATHER: How many questions?

SAM: Sorry.

FATHER: How many you got? Look at the tits on that. Yes, I want to.

For a long time SAM stares at the TV. They don't speak. His stare continues over at least part of the following.

SAM: I love Shelley. *(Pause.)* I really love her. Maybe that's it, Mr Donnelly. Maybe that's everything. Even if she's got chlamydia. And it's not mine. We can overcome that. Love can. It can overcome something like chlamydia.

FATHER: Her mother had that.

SAM: Yes, I know.

Beat.

FATHER: This is my house.

SAM: Yes, I know.

FATHER: This is my house.

SAM: Yes.

FATHER: This is my TV, this is my chair, this is my Bart Simpson mug.

SAM: *(Beat.)* Do you know where Shelley is, Mr Donnelly? *(Beat.)* I need to speak to her.

FATHER: So speak to her.

SAM: Where is she?

FATHER: Don't you know?

SAM: No.

FATHER: Why are you making this my problem?

SAM: I've … I've had such a hard day, I –

FATHER: I don't want to know. This is my house.

SAM: I know that I feel –

FATHER: Don't.

SAM: Mr Donnelly, I am –

FATHER: Don't. *(Beat.)* Look at that bitch. Look at that.

SAM: *(Shouts.)* Shelley! Shelley? Shelley are you there? Shelley?

FATHER starts to rub his crotch. SAM catches sight of this.

SAM: Oh fuck. No – fuck.

SAM exits. The FATHER walks towards the TV which emits a strong coloured light. He reaches into it. SHELLEY seems to emerge from it.

SHELLEY: Dad.

They take each others hands and walk offstage.

THE CONFESSIONAL

SAM flits to the church of earlier.

SAM: *(Shouts.)* Gloria! Gloria. Gloria? I've come back. Need to talk Gloria. Bit of a mess. It's all a mess and I just wanted a clear sign. I went out into the night all open and I felt brave about it but … Not sure what's happening. At all. Gloria it felt good when we were talking. *(Screams out.)* Gloria!

VOICE: Hello?

SAM: Hello?

VOICE: Hello – I heard you. Gloria isn't here now.

SAM: She's not?

VOICE: No, she's got a life you see.

SAM: I saw the poster outside.

VOICE: The poster is good isn't it?

SAM: It made me want to come in.

VOICE: Well done our poster. Good old poster.

SAM: Did Gloria come in like me? Is that how she got a life? *(Beat.)* Are you the priest. Or reverend or whatever?

VOICE: Whatever.

SAM: I can't see you. Are you –

VOICE: Have you come here to mock?

SAM: No, I'm –

VOICE: Lost probably. Have you come here to worship and beg forgiveness for your various sins? Or confess your sickness and excuse your treachery, gather sympathy for your crass life? Seek direction or erections? What lies should we start with? *(Pause.)* You can join this debate at any point you wish. Or are you really not there? Am I talking to an empty place? Is there no one there? Is there no one there? No one? Is no one there? No one? Is no one there? *(Beat.)* Is there –

SAM: Is this a trick?

VOICE: I don't know. I haven't been feeling well.

SAM: Ok.

VOICE: No, not ok. That doesn't help does it? Even though, where I'm at, is a sore head. What have you come here with?

SAM: I've come alone.

VOICE: You've come with nothing?

SAM: I've come for answers, mister, I've been out there and it started with a miracle and you'd think that it would be likely that if the day started with a miracle that the day might be a – a – an astounding day, a bright light of a day, earth turning, world changing, me changing day –

VOICE: Want want want.

SAM: What?

VOICE: Nothing.

SAM: So I came here –

VOICE: Me me me.

SAM: What are you saying?

VOICE: Nothing.

SAM: No come on –

VOICE: Come on.

SAM: If you have something –

VOICE: But you have nothing –

SAM: Then I've come to hear –

VOICE: An empty belly full of eels –

SAM: And that's the beginning isn't it?

VOICE: And in the beginning was the –

SAM: Like Mary – the word made flesh. And the house in the story of Mary is in my house. And I don't know why. And that's why I came here. But you weren't here. And

I met Gloria. It says outside to enter so I did. I am up for whatever the journey is, whatever the meaning and however terrifying I will hold onto it, I will follow the thread. What's it all about?

VOICE: I've no idea. I wish I had. I wish I had answers to these questions: they are reasonable and plain and it distresses me, but right now, right here, right now – can't get in there, there's some pylon has crashed and there's just sparks and a jangly bewilderment.

SAM: I don't want a jangly bewilderment.

VOICE: Well no one would want that would they?

SAM: To fuck with jangly bewilderment!

VOICE: Yes! Yes! To fuck with the jangly bewilderment!

SAM: Fuck it!

VOICE: Fuck it! Fuck it! Fuck. It.

Pause.

SAM: I didn't have time to wash this morning.

VOICE: Ah well.

SAM: I smell of fish. It's coming off me. No idea why. Like dead fish. What does that mean?

VOICE: That doesn't sound good, my friend.

SAM: No. How do you smell?

VOICE: Me? Oh right. The smell of me-ness…? I have to say there is one part of me has to tell you it is a fragrance-less place as if darkness had turned up smelling of something. But part of me also wants to tell you that it smells very bad.

SAM: I can hear you.

VOICE: What?

SAM: It's – you're near.

VOICE: Can you –

SAM: You're just – there's a door.

VOICE: Don't come through the door.

SAM: Why?

VOICE: Don't come through the door. Please.

SAM: Don't –

VOICE: Don't come through the door.

SAM: Why?

VOICE: I don't know.

SAM: What is this?

VOICE: You just need to know it. It's not safe.

SAM: In what way?

VOICE: There's nothing in here for you.

SAM: Are you in there?

VOICE: I don't know.

SAM thinks about opening door.

VOICE: *(Quiet.)* Don't do it.

SAM: That's enough. Now that's just enough. You stop that now, you just stop that.

VOICE: I've seen you.

SAM cries.

VOICE: Is that cr –

He sings a song, hymn, gentle, low, children's song, banal song.

VOICE: Did that comfort you?

SAM: I don't know.

VOICE: Yes you do.

SAM: What?

VOICE: Yes you do.

SAM: No – yes. I think so.

VOICE: How frightening for you not to know what comforts you.

SAM: Who are you?

VOICE: I'm not feeling all that well. Fuzzy. Why were you crying?

SAM: I feel bad. *(Tries to phone.)* No signal. Can't get a signal I came here to be transformed, find divine passage with the glorious vision of being replaced or the rediscovery of forgotten roots of an emerging star to muzzle my disorientation toward a light worth moving for or at least a film of clarity to my confusion and then the next – the – the – the next moment instead of lift off or lid off or lay off even I am captured into an unmoving, hideous blank canvas of, of – and you are here and suddenly, suddenly this – and I don't know why you're here but you are and you know why you're here and it's making me so nervous … You hear me? Why are You here?

VOICE: That's nothing to do with you.

SAM: I'd like to know.

VOICE: This is God's house.

SAM: I know that!

VOICE: Why are you here?

SAM: Tried to –

VOICE: Forget it. You can go now.

SAM moves to open door.

VOICE: No. *(Beat.)* No. *(Beat.)* No. It's not here. It's not here.

SAM exits. There is the sound of GLORIA talking in Polish. Whispers. Indistinguishable. Perhaps a flash of the earlier 'This has to stop.' Then low-key sound of loveless sex.

9. IN THE PARK WITH JACKIE AND JOHNNY

SAM flits to the park. Distant noises. Dogs barking. SAM on the phone.

SAM: Shelley? Shelley? Look, please answer my calls I know you must be picking them up. Look, it's not right to come into my dental appointment and behave like that. I mean how could you do that? I don't get it. I'm so low I feel I'm falling out of myself. I'm in the park – I'm cutting through to go to my Granddad's please call. I don't feel good. I'm in the park. What am I doing in the park? Well I'm in the park and whatever happens is –

Suddenly a MAN and a WOMAN throw themselves into the space. They each have each other by the hair like a school fight so they both face head down like a two-person rugby scrum as they try to kick each other.

JOHNNY: Fuckin' let go.

JACKIE: Let go you.

JOHNNY: I've told you, let go.

JACKIE: Fuckin' let go.

JOHNNY: Who's that?

JACKIE: What?

JOHNNY: There's somebody there.

JACKIE: Who is?

JOHNNY: Somebody.

JACKIE: *(To SAM.)* Who's there?

JOHNNY: Fuckin' own up – who's there?

JACKIE: Are you a cop?

SAM: No.

JACKIE: He's not a cop.

JOHNNY: I could hear him fuckin' idiot.

JACKIE: Cunt.

This kicks off a bout of hair pulling and kicking.

SAM: What are you doing? Just stop.

JACKIE: You tell him that – he started it.

JOHNNY: That's a laugh.

JACKIE: You're an animal.

JOHNNY: At least I'm alive.

JACKIE: I've got problems, Johnny.

JOHNNY: Fucking vampire.

JACKIE: I'm leaving you.

JOHNNY: Good – go then. You won't last.

JACKIE: You got me into all this. It's your fault.

JOHNNY: So go then.

JACKIE: Let go then.

JOHNNY: You let go first. *(To SAM.)* Who are you?

SAM: I'm just Sam.

JOHNNY: Sam, Sam, Sam, don't know any Sam. *(To JACKIE.)* Do you know any Sam?

JACKIE: How the fuck should I know any Sam. Cunt.

SAM: Look, can I ask you what this is all about?

JOHNNY: No, you fucking can't.

JACKIE: Interfering bastard.

JOHNNY: Just keep your nose out, right.

SAM: How did this all start? This is – it's mad.

Over the following they try to find SAM without letting go of each others' hair.

JOHNNY: Mad – ya prick –

JACKIE: Fuckin' little –

JOHNNY: Comes out of nowhere and –

JACKIE: Patronising cunt –

JOHNNY: Where are you, ya – ?

JACKIE: Fuckin' discover yourself ya –

SAM: *(Shouts, angry.)* I've got problems too!

JOHNNY: Who said we've got problems?

SAM: She did.

JACKIE: *She* did? *She* did? Who's *she?* The cat's mother.

JOHNNY: That's my wife you're talking about.

SAM: I didn't mean any disrespect.

JACKIE: *She? She's* got a name.

SAM: What's your name?

JACKIE: Jackie. That's Johnny.

SAM: Sam.

JOHNNY: Fuckin' know your name. Who asked you your name?

SAM: Nobody.

JOHNNY: Cheeky cunt.

SAM: Look, I'm going to go and leave you to it.

They disengage from their violent embrace.

JOHNNY: Not yet.

SAM: Not yet?

JACKIE: I'm going to massacre him if he keeps that up.

JOHNNY: What you up to?

SAM: Up – I was heading up to my Granddad's.

JOHNNY: He live in the park?

SAM: No. What was all that about?

JOHNNY: All what?

SAM: All that.

They both look at SAM. They get lost in recollection.

JOHNNY: Can't remember.

JACKIE: No.

JOHNNY: Isn't that mad?

JACKIE: What is that about?

JOHNNY: Mental.

JACKIE: Absolutely mental.

JACKIE stares at SAM.

JACKIE: I know you.

SAM: Don't think so.

JACKIE: How do I know you?

JOHNNY: What's going on here, then?

JACKIE: I know him.

JOHNNY: She knows you.

SAM: No, no I don't think so.

JACKIE: I recognize him, Johnny.

JOHNNY: What you up to?

SAM: Nothing, I told you I was –

JACKIE: Fuck! *(Looks at her phone.)* It's him.

JOHNNY: What?

JACKIE: It's him – the guy – remember?

JOHNNY: What guy?

JACKIE: The guy – look.

Show him the phone. They look at it and stare.

JOHNNY: That's the guy.

JACKIE: That's what I said. You saw a girl this morning right? Wee girl – pink dress, twelve years old?

JOHNNY: She's fucking eleven?

JACKIE: How do you know?

SAM: Yes?

JOHNNY: Our Julie.

SAM: How did you –

JACKIE: Cause your on Facebook. You're on my phone. She sent the alert out.

SAM: Oh God.

JOHNNY: Were you looking at our Julie's tits?

SAM: No, I didn't.

JOHNNY: But I've got proof here.

SAM: How can that be proof?

JACKIE: That you?

SAM: Yes, but –

JOHNNY hits him. JACKIE hits him too.

SAM: I've got a girlfriend. Well she's – we're having problems but –

JOHNNY: What age is she?

SAM: She's – I think she's …

JACKIE: See that?

JOHNNY: He's making it up. There's fuck all girlfriend.

JACKIE: Didn't expect to meet her mum and dad in the park though did you?

Beat.

SAM: No.

JACKIE: Otherwise he wouldn't have done it would he?

JOHNNY: Didn't think it through did you big man?

SAM: I didn't do anything.

JOHNNY: Where have we heard that before, eh? Confess. Confess motherfucker.

SAM: Confess what?

JOHNNY hits him again.

JACKIE: Fucking cheek coming into our park after what he did.

SAM: I didn't do anything.

JACKIE: In our fucking park.

SAM: It's *not* your park – it's my park too!

JACKIE: Fuckin' wants our park, Johnny.

JOHNNY: Un-fucking-believable.

JACKIE: So where we supposed to go then? Just fuck off somewhere?

JOHNNY: So where then?

JACKIE: Fuckin' molests our daughtger then steals our park.

SAM: The park is for sharing.

JOHNNY: Like my daughter you mean?

SAM: I didn't touch her!

JACKIE: This is a nightmare, Johnny.

JOHNNY: I can't believe this is happening.

SAM: Nothing's happening.

JOHNNY: Think you have nothing then they find something else to take from you, like something you forgot you had.

JACKIE: This can't be happening.

JOHNNY: Fuck me.

JACKIE: Give us our fucking park back!

SAM: What are you on about? You're scaring the shit out of me.

JOHNNY: Fuckin' straight up – give us it back! Now!

SAM: I've not got your park.

JOHNNY: Where you fucking standing then, pisshead, answer me that?

JACKIE: Come on – where are you?

JOHNNY: Where are you fuckin' –

SAM: In the park.

JOHNNY: In the park. In the park. He admits it.

JACKIE: Look at him just standing there.

SAM: *(Loud, suddenly.)* Help! Help! *(Beat.)* Please, I'm really sorry. I haven't done anything.

JOHNNY: Prove it.

SAM: How can I prove it?

JACKIE: He's fucking lying Johnny.

JOHNNY: Shut up, Jackie

JACKIE: No, you shut up.

SAM: Listen to me – I haven't – I haven't done anything. Nothing. *(Beat.)* I'm just the same as you. Just the same. I've got nothing.

JACKIE: What you mean the same as us? What does he mean by that?

SAM: I don't mean you any harm. I only wanted to help you.

JACKIE: Fuckin' words.

JOHNNY: Yeah.

JACKIE: Get a fuckin' brick Johnny.

JOHNNY looks for a brick. Woman takes out a crack cigarette, sits down.

JOHNNY: You better not fuckin' finish that off. That the last?

JACKIE: I'm stressed out – just a wee bit and I'll be fine, Johnny.

JOHNNY: Don't finish that, right?

JACKIE: I'm not.

JOHNNY: Ok then. Because I'm out there looking for bricks for us. *(Beat.)* You better not fucking finish that.

JACKIE: I'm just taking a bit, Johnny.

JOHNNY: Just make fuckin' sure right Jackie.

JACKIE: All right. Have you found a brick yet, Johnny?

JOHNNY: I'm just going right.

JACKIE: Right then.

JOHNNY exits looking for bricks. JACKIE takes a puff of the crack fag, takes out an inhaler, uses it and then takes another draw of the fag.

SAM: Is that drugs?

JACKIE: What?

SAM: I'm not judging or anything. I'm open to anything. Specially today.

JACKIE: Oh you're open to anything, are you?

SAM: Yes.

JACKIE: Are you then. *(Shouts off.)* Johnny, going to hurry up with that brick!

SAM: Yes, Jackie.

JACKIE: So you – who told you my name was Jackie?

SAM: Well he –

JACKIE: This is freaking me right out, man.

SAM: No, Johnny –

JACKIE: You know his name as well? What the fuck is going on here? Who are you? How do you know about us?

SAM: I don't, I –

JACKIE: *(Shouts off.)* Johnny just come back here.

JOHNNY: *(Off.)* I can't find any fucking bricks, just bit of tree fuck.

JACKIE: Forget the bricks!

JOHNNY: How we going to brick him then?

JACKIE: Just come back, Johnny! Johnny!!!

JOHNNY: Ok. Ok.

JACKIE: Don't you move till Johnny comes back, ok.

SAM: This is too much.

JACKIE: Just you stay there because –

There is the noise of a gunshot off. Silence.

JACKIE: Oh God.

SAM: That sounded like …

JACKIE: Have you brought people with you?

SAM: I'm completely alone.

JACKIE: Fuck.

SAM: I'm scared.

JACKIE: *(Hisses.)* Shut up.

There is the sound of whispering voices. A beat. Then the sound of a hammer hitting something, presumably JOHNNY. Some more whispers. The sound of a body being dragged, rustle of bin bag. Sound of dragging. Fades away.

JACKIE: They got him.

SAM: Who?

JACKIE: My lovely Johnny. My darling boy.

SAM: Do you think he's …

JACKIE: Of course he fucking is, fuck.

She lights up crack fag again.

SAM: I'm really sorry.

JACKIE: That doesn't mean anything. How am I going to get more stuff? So where am I now? Am I going somewhere? Where do I go? And Julie. Little Julie …

SAM: I see her in you.

JACKIE: Do you? Do you really? That's lovely. Me and Johnny called her Julie because we were J & J, you know. We liked that. So we made it so it was J & J & J … but that didn't sound as good. But we realized too late and had already signed the birth thing and all that. Do you want some? *(Indicates fag.)*

SAM: Yes.

They smoke.

SAM: What are you going to do?

JACKIE: Probably best run away. Or it could be all right now, you know, with Johnny …

SAM: Right, right. This is amazing by the way. Wow.

She stares at him. He takes another drag. She pulls it abruptly away.

SAM: What have I done?

JACKIE: Nothing. Move. Move away now.

SAM: I want to help you and Julie.

JACKIE: No you don't.

SAM: Yes I do.

JACKIE: Don't trust anyone who wants to help me.

SAM: I mean it. I want to change this for you.

JACKIE: Do you?

SAM: Yes I do.

JACKIE: I'll tell you what then. You wake up tomorrow – if you get out of this park all right – and you still want to do that –

SAM: Ok.

JACKIE: Ok?

SAM: Ok.

JACKIE: So fuck off then.

SAM gets up to go. JACKIE takes inhaler again.

SAM: I'm sorry about Johnny.

JACKIE: Johnny.

SAM: Yeah.

JACKIE: Johnny.

SAM goes to go again.

SAM: Jackie. I never did anything to Julie.

JACKIE: Didn't you?

SAM: I promise. I never even looked at her …

JACKIE: *(Looks at him.)* Didn't you?

A beat. SAM goes. JACKIE stands up, doesn't move, just dangling in space. Exits.

10. GRANDDAD'S DEAD

SAM flits to his grandfather's house. The wheelchair is upturned in a corner. GRANDDAD is in it. The electric motor sets the wheels in motion sporadically. A fly buzzes.

SAM: Granddad? Granddad? Granddad? Granddad? Granddad? Granddad? Granddad. Granddad! Granddad! Granddad! Granddad! Granddad! Granddad! Granddad! Granddad. Granddad. Granddad. Granddad.

SAM sits. Maybe.

Didn't mean to frighten … I'm ok. I'm ok. Yes I am. It's ok granddad. And it's ok that your dead. Although it means that no one will ever talk to me like you talked to me ever again. And it means that all the things you talked about will start to fade. And it means that I won't ever hear the things you haven't said yet that I wanted to know but didn't ask. Because I was talking. Talking. Talking. But it means I can stop feeling guilty about not coming to see you more. And it means I can stop feeling guilty about not cuddling you. And how you were tall and thin even though you were old. And how it felt awkward for me to love you because you were a Nazi. Or a BNP pamphleteer. Even when your legs stopped working. Which must have been hard in a wheelchair because it's hilly around here. Which means you must have meant it. *(Beat.)* You must have meant it. Oh no. Oh no.

I'll take you to see my house, granddad. It's a holy house.

SAM walks over to the wheelchair. Stands.

SAM: I love you granddad. I wish you could open your eyes and see my house. I love you.

SAM goes to pick up the wheelchair and is electrocuted. He jumps around for a bit in pain and shock and recovers, walks over and switches it off and the wheel stops turning. He goes to pick it up again and is again electrocuted. He is dumbfounded. He instinctively kicks the wheelchair a few times. There is a small explosion and crackle and some smoke.

SAM: How can? What is? A sign? A sign?

SAM very tentatively lifts the wheelchair to an upright position revealing GRANDDAD for the first time. His face is black with smoke, like a rough and ready black and white minstrel.

11. THE BUSINESS END OF THINGS

SAM flits to the street pushing his GRANDDAD in the wheelchair. A BUSINESS WOMAN appears in the street. She appears to be about to ask a question of SAM, thinks better of it and moves to leave.

SAM: Wait.

BUSINESS WOMAN: It's all right.

SAM: What is?

BUSINESS WOMAN: 'It' is. All right? Sorry.

SAM: You were going to ask me something.

BUSINESS WOMAN: No, no, it's fine, you just carry on … carry on, whatever. I'll be fine.

SAM: Anything.

BUSINESS WOMAN: What?

SAM: Anything you want to say you can just say it.

BUSINESS WOMAN: Ok.

SAM: Ok.

BUSINESS WOMAN: Where is the Malmaison from here? I'm lost.

SAM: The Malmaison …

BUSINESS WOMAN: You don't know. That's fine. Thanks anyway.

SAM: I might.

BUSINESS WOMAN: No, you don't. It's all right. It's all right not to know where the Malmaison is.

SAM: You here on business?

BUSINESS WOMAN: Yes I am. Only reason I'd ever come back to this shithole.

SAM: What kind of business?

BUSINESS WOMAN: Can we end this now?

SAM: Why?

BUSINESS WOMAN: Because now it's you who wants something and I don't want to give it. Do taxis exist here?

SAM: What do I want?

BUSINESS WOMAN: You want to talk. Or maybe tell me your life-story or spill the beans about your traumatic evening. It was traumatic wasn't it?

SAM: Yes.

BUSINESS WOMAN: There we are – you wear your need like a Royal Ascot hat and that and your general appearance makes my heart sink into gut turning drains with the near certainty that your story of your evening or life will never fit into the 'happy story' shelf. And me? I'm pissed off and a bit pissed and in no mood to indulge your dispiriting need to share what is un-sharable – that is the uniquely human experience of being *you. (Beat.)* I'm sorry if that's harsh.

SAM: This is my Granddad.

BUSINESS WOMAN: Well, not a good listener are we? You, unlike me, have not spent several hours tuning your active listening skills in a managing difficult people workshop.

SAM: No.

BUSINESS WOMAN: Thought so. I did. Today. Lots of active listening. It was so active that I became exhausted and compelled to take refuge in a violent and highly active bout of shopping. Shopping, I like shopping. You get what you pay for. You don't negotiate, the value's the value and hey, there it is on the price tag – a nice, brutal clarity and I can make it happen and the end result is a real orgasm because it is getting something for 'me.' And I like that. Everybody does. It makes 'me' happier than before. Oh yes, definitely.

SAM: You had a hard day too then?

BUSINESS WOMAN: Yes, yes, I have. Look, I thought I saw your story coming up there – remember don't fuck with my drains. *(Beat.)* Ok, ok, I'll say it now so you don't hate me – fuck it, I don't care if you hate me, why should I – but anyway, nice to meet you and your Granddad, so let's end it all there, shall we – where are the taxis in this shithole –

SAM: My Granddad's dead.

BUSINESS WOMAN: He's what?

SAM: He's dead.

BUSINESS WOMAN: Right. He's dead right? *(SAM nods.)* Are you taking him to the hospital?

SAM: He's dead – you can't fix that at a hospital, they can't cure the dead there.

BUSINESS WOMAN: That's true. Isn't that what you do anyway?

SAM: I don't know – this is my first death.

BUSINESS WOMAN: Mine too. Well he's not my Granddad, but … You need to phone someone.

SAM: Who?

BUSINESS WOMAN: There'll be someone you can phone and they'll take care of it.

SAM: Take care of what?

BUSINESS WOMAN: 'It.' Someone will do it all. Might do a taxi service where they come and pick them up. *(Beat.)* Maybe they could drop me off at the Malmaison. Sorry – insensitive. Look, you can't go wheeling a dead person round the streets like this.

SAM: I'm taking him home.

BUSINESS WOMAN: And then?

SAM: We have a holy house there.

BUSINESS WOMAN: You do know that with the *(Indicates blood and marks on his face.)* you might well look like the murderer of your dead grandfather.

SAM: Oh.

BUSINESS WOMAN: *(Nervous suddenly.)* Did you?

SAM: No, I loved him.

BUSINESS WOMAN: I'm sorry.

SAM: Yeah.

BUSINESS WOMAN: That's shitty.

SAM: Yeah.

BUSINESS WOMAN: At least he was old.

SAM: Yeah.

BUSINESS WOMAN: How old was he?

SAM: You know, I don't know – I don't know what age my Granddad was.

BUSINESS WOMAN: Don't worry, no one ever knows what age old people are: it stops mattering after a point. I'm on a team building weekend. And I've lost the rest of my team. Oops.

SAM: Have you got their –

BUSINESS WOMAN: Now why did I tell you that? I knew you'd do this. I can't stand being around people like you.

SAM: Why?

BUSINESS WOMAN: You're messy. You mess up stuff. Oh wrong – shouldn't have said that – Oh fuck it I'm on holiday, well nearly, might as well be –

SAM: How did you just turn like that, I've been out all day and –

BUSINESS WOMAN: Can I stop you just there before you do my drains in. You're messy. I mean this is the twenty-first

century, why should I have to encounter someone like you
– and that – on the street?

SAM: I live here, actually. I actually live here.

BUSINESS WOMAN: Do you, actually. Actually 'live?' What's
your tribe?

SAM: Tribe?

BUSINESS WOMAN: Come on, yes, what's your tribe – who
do you belong to? You see I'm part of a big powerful and
energetic twenty-first century legion that's about making
things faster, better, cheaper, more available, more
ordered, smoother, longer, harder, cleverer, more accurate,
sustainable, healthier, safer, forward-looking – think five
years – resilient, transparent, clearer, more affordable,
more accountable, flexible, reliable, replaceable,
appropriately resourced, brand defined, well-connected,
more relevant, international but locally minded, supported
by rigorous maps of systems and processes, keeping up to
date with the future yet to come at the touch of a button,
always open to feedback and input and inspirational. And
whilst I embark on all of this well here you are wheeling
your dead grandfather around fucking Baltic sidestreets
looking like a geek's faded video of 'Steptoe and Son'.

SAM: At least I know where I am. I want to hit you, I do. I
want to hit you with an answer that will just knock you
over, you 'cock.' I'm going home how. Good luck with the
team building.

BUSINESS WOMAN: I don't need luck. Luck's the lazy man's
mysticism.

SAM: Goodbye.

BUSINESS WOMAN: Natural selection should probably do it
eventually. *(Seeing a taxi off.)* Taxi! Thank fuck! Take me …
(Under breath.) away from here.

BUSINESS WOMAN exits. Sound of the children from the first half, off.

GIRL: Hey look – it's the paedo.

BOY: *(Like football chant.)* Paedo. Paedo.

SAM: Stop that. I need to speak to you.

GIRL: Hey mister – you're famous now, how's that?

BOY: Paedo.

SAM: It's about your – .

Sound of children's laughter fades into distance. SAM tries his phone.

SHELLEY: *(Voice.)* Hello, it's me Shelley. Sorry can't speak *(Muffled.)* A minute dad. Sorry can't speak right now but you can leave a mssage. Wait for the beep. Here it comes

… Here. it comes. *(Beeps.)*

SAM doesn't speak.

12. SAM'S FINAL HOMECOMING

SAM flits back to the house with GRANDDAD in his wheelchair. It is quiet. He goes to the wall, touches it.

SAM: Oh you. You now. Take me with you. Go on. Take me. Flit away, I don't mind. I'll hang on. Flit flit. I don't think you can stay here. I'm sorry. I went out and it didn't happen. I still don't know. Anything. Anything. It doesn't matter. It's a mess, don't like it, don't want it. It's ugly. It's just ugly. We're ugly. Flit flit. Any time you like.

MUM: *(Croaky voiced.)* Son?

SAM: How did that happen? How? I mean there's everything: food, water, electricity, nearly everyone's got a roof, loads have got sky dishes on them, cheap flights to Bari. How come we're not … How come I'm not happy?

DAD: *(Big.)* A big disappointment. You're a disappointment!

MUM: Don't pay any heed: dad is, well he's not doing so well. *(To DAD.)* Engage brain before – before – erm, saying something, like that. Mmm.

A VOICE howls offstage, it is aggressive and emotional, indistinguishable words.

SAM: Is that dad?

MUM: No son, that's not dad.

The VOICE arcs over the space plaintive now and ending with an, 'Oh fucking hell – save us.'

SAM: That's not dad.

DAD: Son.

MUM: That's your dad, now don't try to speak.

SAM: Dad?

DAD: *(Shouts.)* I'm hungry.

SAM: Me too.

DAD: I'm fucking hungry.

MUM: Dad!

DAD: I'm hungry! I'm hungry!

SAM: I know dad.

DAD: Give me some food. I'm fucking hungry.

SAM: I'm so fucking hungry.

DAD: I'm hungry.

SAM: So hungry.

DAD: *(Crying.)* I'm hungry.

MUM: Now don't start that.

SAM: I know dad.

DAD: I'm hungry.

MUM: Just stop it will you. Stop it now please.

DAD is just crying.

SAM: Mum, what am I for? *(Pause.)* Here I am. I'm ready. I promise I won't be difficult. There's things happening out there mum and it's just happening and it's like the things don't know why they're happening either: didn't want me to add or join up. Nothing. And I feel ashamed of that nothing. And I feel ashamed of *it*. I'm ashamed of *you*.

MUM: Don't …

SAM: And I'm ashamed of feeling ashamed of you.

MUM: Don't now son. You're not happy.

SAM: That's true. That's very true.

MUM: We all just have to get on with it.

SAM: No, that's not true, that's not good enough. We don't.

MUM: You'll just make yourself more unhappy.

SAM: Why has this miracle happened to me?

MUM: Now about that.

More maniacal laughter, howling and growling from off.

SAM: What *is* that Mum?

MUM: Well, that's the thing, your miracle.

SAM: What are those noises to do with that?

MUM: That's Gordon.

SAM: Gordon?

MUM: Yes, that's Gordon you can hear. Well, you know the wall.

SAM: The wall of the holy house, yeah.

MUM: And how it flitted to here, in our house.

SAM: Yeah.

MUM: On top of your dad. Well, it's not like that.

DAD: *(Faint.)* Don't, mum, don't –

MUM: He needs to know.

SAM: Know what?

MUM: It's not the holy house.

SAM: It *is* the holy house.

MUM: There's no miracle.

SAM: It's there! It's right in front of us, mum. We heard it on the news. It disappeared. For the first time in seven hundred years the house of Mary disappeared from its place in Loreto.

More indistinguishable shouting from GORDON.

MUM: But only for half a minute.

SAM: What do you mean?

MUM: And only on the TV.

SAM: On TV?

MUM: It was all an illusion, son. For TV Derren Brown made it disappear last night. I think Gordon said one in four people saw it disappear … if you know what I mean.

SAM: Gordon said that?

MUM: When him not having alcohol really kicked in – before the serious DTing started.

More from GORDON.

MUM: Anyway he can't really talk now. He's in a cupboard, I think he said. It's awful. And his dog's trapped in a disused boiler. He thinks it's broken its leg. It's the upstairs wall, son. All the support's gone and the wall must have, well I don't know, I'm not a builder.

SAM: It's just a wall?

MUM: Just a wall son, I'm sorry.

SAM: But how can it be just a wall?

MUM: It's just a wall, son.

SAM: It was so wonderful. That something cut through my world, something that wasn't there before, from nowhere and was … a light. Beautiful light sharp and clear and certain. And I would see myself. And maybe see myself as beautiful, mum. Mum, I really, really wanted to feel beautiful. It was like a breath passed through me and filled me up, mum. You know. No miracle here. Where is it gone? Where is it? I can't see it. Where's it gone? I can't … It's just … But I don't know where it is. I don't know. And it can't cure dad now like it did those people, can it. It can't. All it is, is a wall. Can't help dad's legs now.

SAM exits.

MUM: Sam? Sam, where are you. Go and get someone, son. We need to sort this out.

Dog howling.

MUM: I'm not sure how much longer your dad can hold out. It's getting to that point. Son?

SAM returns. He has a chainsaw. He revs up. GORDON goes hysterical next door. Cuts out.

MUM: Is that the chainsaw, son. Listen don't try anything silly. Don't try and be a hero, it'll only break or worse, it could break the brick. Think about that. Could bring the whole thing down on us.

SAM revs it up once more and he moves over to his DAD's legs. GORDON goes crazy next door. He hovers above his legs thinking about sawing them off. He hovers. He puts it off. A silence.

MUM: Son? *(Beat.)* Son? *(Beat.)* Son, where are you? Are you still there?

SAM: Yes.

Flash of light. Blackout.

Mark has been Artistic Director of the Royal Lyceum Theatre Company since April 2003 during which time he has directed, amongst others, Shakespeare's *The Winter's Tale, Julius Caesar, Othello, As You Like It* and *The Merchant of Venice*; Oscar Wilde's *The Importance of Being Earnest*; Pirandello's *Six Characters in Search of an Author* (a co-production with the National Theatre of Scotland and the Citizens Theatre); premieres of Jo Clifford's *Every One* and Goethe's *Faust, Parts One and Two*; *Six Black Candles* and *Monks* by Des Dillon and John Byrne's *Uncle Varick* and his own plays *A Madman Sings to the Moon*, his adaptation of James Hogg's *The Private Memoirs and Confessions of a Justified Sinner* and Carlo Collodi's *Pinocchio*.

Mark was Artistic Director of the Brunton Theatre Company from 1997–2002, directing 21 shows, winning a Herald Angel Award for his play *A Madman Sings to the Moon* and a Scotsman Fringe First and a Herald Angel Award for his play *Moving Objects*. He was Assistant Director at the Theatre Royal Stratford East and the Royal Shakespeare Company and Associate Director at Nottingham Playhouse.

Mark was born and brought up in Harthill in Lanarkshire. He arrived in Edinburgh via Glasgow, London, Stratford (East and on Avon) and Nottingham, where he lives with his partner Megan and children Harry and Millie.